Juanita,
You are my ?
Strength. Keep
I need; pray for your own
happiness. Thank you for
being the unique you God
created you to be.

Abused No More
"The Breaking Of A Mindset"

Love,
Yours "Marie"

Book Development & Editing
Coach B Write For Me LLC
CoachBWriteForMe@Gmail.Com
www.HelpMeCoachB.Org

Front Cover Design
Dr. Joyce Hatcher
jrawlshatcher@beulahland.org

Mission Statement

The mission of LaTrice Marie is to equip readers and followers with divine wisdom and understanding that no matter what their current situation, God is still able and willing to deliver.

He is the king that resides within us, and still performing the same miracles that we read about in the Bible.
It is our responsibility to reach out and receive what He is offering.

It is my goal to inspire and instill greatness that will result in deliberate actions, plans and focus on becoming who we were purposed to be.

I aim to ignite a fire that will allow us to bless others through mentoring and motivating our youth.

For I am a true believer, and I acknowledge that we are indeed, our brothers' and sisters' keepers…

Table Of Contents

Dedication

I dedicate this book to Toledo, Ohio. To every girl and boy who have always been told that they couldn't but in fact would at the appointed time, I hear you. To those of you who missed hearing, "I love you" consistently, or when they needed it the most, I feel you. To every person who has been called everything but your real name in a home that harvested defeated, conniving spirits, I implore you to step out and create the change that we all need.

To those individuals who gave their heart to the point of exhaustion with nothing left to retrieve from leech-like spirits sucking everything that sustains you dry, I see you. To men and woman alike, that were told that you were ugly and believed it, I challenge you to see yourself as the much-needed gift that only you can bring to this earth. To you all, when told that you are pretty, feel that it is either a setup or figure of speech, know that it is not. Learn to trust your initial instincts (God endowed you with them) about the persons that you allow to encompass your personal space. To everyone out there that has gone to "your dad's" family function and consistently heard, "now you know, that (not he or she) isn't his child," and still somehow remained naive for quite some time, you are not empty nor are you alone.

To each of you that feel as though you have experienced the worst and still have the audacity to expect and be at your best daily, this book is dedicated to you.

May I remind you that I do this for you, believing that one day the last will be a consistent first. That day is today, and I have a new declaration. We are the first to win and maintain the victory. We are the first to give our all in a sincere praise and worship knowing that it is already well, deep within our souls.

We are first to give, show and proclaim our love to our brothers and sisters (period) in a nature that is both genuine and unselfish. To those of you who feel unloved, unworthy, unattractive, vanished or buried alive with suffocation as your breath, this is no longer thy truth. Release it like your very life depends on it! Because it does. Know that at this very moment, I love you like I need you to be successful and joyous upon each occasion that you are faced with, for you and I are one.

We have shaken loose the shackles that have bound us in the past. We are here now and have been heard upon arrival because we do indeed matter. Our dreams have manifested and materialized because we have realized who we are in HIM. And as we surrender, our eyes are now wired wide open and our tears have become muted. The taste of dysentery thought patterns have dissipated and YOU are all that remains.

I thank you Lord, for never leaving nor forsaking me when YOU had every reason to abandon me! I have been a self-imploding, disobedient wreckage of a ship. I surrender as I float effortlessly because of all that You are to and for me. I will forever praise your name! Selah.

To my loving husband, Trevone, children Roderick (Timmi), Robynn and Johnny, I love you more than my words can announce. To my grandson, Romerius, that brings me so much joy, you were my strength even before you could speak. To Rochelle (Dexter), Juanita, Momma

Elianne Vertus, Erica, Nicolette (Chad), Kathryn Campbell, Jessica Denicola, Tasha Greene, Super Nova a.k.a Liz, Pastor Berneka Alleyne, Nycholle Gater and Tracy (Nacherel Sparks) Staten, I am in awe of the way God has strategically placed each of you in my life for a time such as this. Your words have encouraged, motivated and propelled me into a position to praise, receive and count it all joy. For this reason, I thank you and praise God for the many blessings He has bestowed upon me through you.

I am forever grateful as He is worthy to be praised. In addition, I would like to give a special thank you. Pastor Joyce Hatcher, I appreciate, love and marvel at your work. You are such an abundant blessing, an anointed gift and a rare find. Thank you for your many gifts, especially the one that allowed you to see the vision (cover) even better than I.

To Pastor Steve at U-turn for Christ (Tennessee), your efforts will never be in vain nor have they gone unseen...

Chapter One
"INTRODUCTION"

Who am I? I am very simple yet heavily complicated. I am a wife, mother, grandmother, daughter, sister to many, friend and love one that intends to nurture all that I am blessed to come into contact with. Most importantly, I am a believer.

It just so happens that at one point, I identified myself as broken beyond repair. My walk was a direct reflection of this on the daily. I mirrored multiple hardships, lack, self-destruction and contempt, most of the time, without awareness or even speaking a word. Through this epic journey in life, I have learned a great many lessons that I would love to teach and share with you. As a young woman, I now look back at the girl that started being penetrated at three years of age.

I now see innocence planted on a battlefield wandering in and out of the enemy's territory unarmed, unprepared, unprotected and unaware of the dangers that she would face, swallow and wear like a badge of honor. Nowadays, I can cry freely for the weight that she sustained on her shoulders for a lifetime, never belonged to her. However, they left their hideous markings all the same. Never having a consistent father or protective figure in my life, allowed me to easily be receptive to the lies being taught (both spoken and unspoken alike). I began to not only flourish but self-propel in the cesspool of the most crippling yet comforting hatred possible- the one labeled as self. Everything about LaTrice, I hated and would have changed within a heartbeat.

I internalized and devoured this as the only truth that I would ever know and clung to it to the point of death (spiritual, mental and physical too). My life choices echoed that death on every spiral and turn that I invested in. I committed myself to the familiar cycle of failure, regret, abuse, poverty, etc., rather than taking the risk of being happy, which was unfamiliar, unpredictable and unattractive to me. During those years, I loathed taking pictures as they always seemed to expose what I was truly wearing beneath the superficial smile. Misery.

Others could never seem to understand the choices that I made or me. I remained loyal in an abusive, non-committed (on his behalf) relationship for eight years. I was never ignorant of this fact, just accepting to the point of numbness. As a matter of fact, it began to harden my heart to such emotionlessness that in order for me to be able to achieve or manipulate crying, I had to physically do what I had done spiritually and mentally to myself for years. I chose to self-mutilate in one of the lowest degrees.

The pain that I experienced during those festivities felt just as levitating and amazing as it was addictive. I became "plenty of tattoos and body piercings" to win pain for no other rhyme or reason than I simply needed to cry, be heard, feel alive and relieve the numbness monopolizing my heart. But God! In His beautiful, unique and perfected timing brought me out of the darkness distracting, detaining and debilitating me into His glorious splendor. He has endowed me to bless and equip you.

Over time, He has shown me the error in my miscalculated ways and steps, which derived from my false belief systems. He has shown me that I was not the mirror of my past (abuse, mistakes, bad decisions, cycles, etc.) neither are you. Contrarily, we were made in His image, loved and wanted immeasurably as well as being fearfully and wonderfully made (in every shape, shade and mental capacity). As I wrote my first book, "Wounded," He showed me first, that He was always there. Secondly, He spoke the words, "Ordered," upon my heart.

This meant that everything that I had experienced: good, bad, the reactions to my disobedience and excluded nothing, had been ordained or permitted by God to be used at a later time for His Glory. Praise God! As you know, this view alone was more than sufficient; it can be likened to His grace that covers and makes us whole. This word, ordered, was a ground-shaking revelation and the Rhema word (God-inspired and relating to the present situations that we face) that satisfied my thirst. However, He could have but chose not to leave it at that.

He left me with a "knowing" in my spirit and etched upon my heart that this was not the final lesson that He would teach me pertaining to the book that He blessed me to write. This notion easily transcends into my life lessons as well. As a matter of fact, in a vision on December 30th of 2018, I saw Jesus. And at that very moment, He saved my life in more ways than one. He confirmed all that I thought I knew but was uncertain of. He looked me in my eyes and spoke "Encourager," and I silently nodded my head.

This is my gift but more importantly, His command. He showed me the end product (this book and others to come) in order for me to be fruitful. Without explaining the process, price or struggles that would attempt to decapitate me spiritually. He led me on a path of righteousness for His namesake. Because of this, I am in active pursuit to fulfill my purpose for this lifetime. I write this book in an effort to be made transparent in order to save souls versus sell books.

I do this not to win fans by exposing or condemning others. My heart's desire is to freely give the love that He has faithfully shown towards me. I intend to share the type of love that will: require you to change your current viewpoint, look towards Him, evolve beyond your highest limitation and live in expectancy, the life of abundance thus saith the Lord. This is truly my ultimate goal. The selling of books will come and is secondary in nature to me.

This leaves me with no other alternative than to trust Him in totality. In doing so, I will continue to progress forward in faith moves so colossal that command the mountains of poverty, abuse, sickness and the like to be not only canceled but uncreated in Jesus' name. I recommend that you do the same. I pray that this book not only blesses you but prepares, restores and equips you to not only face the storms surrounding you, but allows you to come out from that storm better than you were before. My prayer is that this book shall unlock the mysteries that may have caused you to drift, settle, be chained or harbor unforgiveness to be broken into bits in Jesus' name.

I implore the Lord to allow this book to break the mindset of abuse and any other cycle that leads to living a life malignant and less than His best for your life in Jesus' name.

Amen.

Chapter Two
"Dilapidated Foundation"

In today's society, we believe and tend to lean on the fact that we can do all things and find all solutions by asking. This principle was established Biblically, which means that it can be proven and will emphatically withstand the test of time. Therefore, the only problem that I can fathom at this point is that we are continuously running toward Google to find the solutions instead of chasing after God as we were in fact created to do. With that being said and a slight sense of sarcasm, I too have used Google in an effort to define the meaning of the word dilapidated. According to Google, dilapidated is a term that is used to describe the state of a building or object that is in despair or ruin as a result of age or neglect.

This definition is not only true physically but can also be applied spiritually as well. But before we begin to characterize the meaning of dilapidation in the spiritual sense, let's dig a bit deeper. I'll start this portion with a question to be pondered. How would you define the word foundation? In answering this question, I believe that we can all agree that our foundation is one of the most essential parts of any establishment.

In fact, it should be the very first item of construction. Like Genesis, our foundation is the very beginning of our creation (and should in turn promote our growth as well). In an effort to help you visualize the fundamentals of any foundation, in the simplest terms, is to understand that it is the ground level, underlying principle, or concrete structure that is utilized for support. Without a solid, working foundation, we crumble. Insufficient of the defining characteristics as mentioned above, it would be nearly impossible to begin building (upward).

It could be likened to the wasting of much needed time, space and effort, as we would inadvertently be spiraling downward over a period of time. In short, our foundation or our "beginning" should be characteristic of strength, sufficiency and nurturing in the natural and spiritual sense. It must also be built upon trust in order to be effective. We should have a strong faith that our foundation will be able to sustain the extraordinary blows of time. As the ultimate goal, the foundation is what establishes whether or not the building will be able to stand firm and erect under the surmounting pressures of the world.

It will be the determining factor on whether or not the building withstands blunt force opposition (incremental weather, etc.) and remains standing. It is crucial that our foundation be delinquent of cracks, leaks or sloppy and rushed processing of the architecture. Or it will ultimately be the cause for its caving and destruction (whether self-imposed or stemming from position, condition or climate changes). At this point, you may be a little perplexed and wondering what it is that I am leading up to. In short, the building that I keep referring to is not one made of cement nor created or designed by man. I am referring to the original Potter's blessings and giving direct reference to the clay- you and me.

Our foundations are not only the parents we're born to, but also includes the environment that we were planted in and the circumstances that we have been faced with. Trusting that our physical, emotional, spiritual and psychological needs will be met within a timely matter is the key to securing an operative foundation. In essence, our foundation can also be likened to the soil used for gardening. The fertility of that soil or lack thereof that we were planted in, will ultimately demonstrate the type of growth or success that we will inevitably build and create upon. Consequently, if that soil is void of the much-needed nutrients, it will inevitably lead to the withering and decay of even the biggest and best potential.

We must be cognizant of this at all times. In either of these options, whether good or bad, the changes that we experience are a direct correlation to the atmosphere or soil we are afforded.   Changes, due to our conditioning, could happen immediately, or just may progress slowly over time. In a model situation, our foundations would be solid, viewed as beneficial in all aspects by us and easily defined as a blessing by others. To make this a vivid picture is to show both present, loving, financially and emotionally stable parents, hugged up on the couch, cradling and swaddling you in love with hope-filled eyes.

It is to envision your parents daydreaming not only about meeting but surpassing all of your needs as their ultimate goal. It would demonstrate an environment with (little to) no arguments, sibling rivalry or hostility ever. This picture would be free from flaws, hurt and harm. Everyone that we would come into contact with would be beaming with genuine love displays towards us daily. The streets would be saturated with gold from our footfalls into more exceedingly joyful situations to follow.

And as beautiful as this sounds, it is not realistic. More often times than not, this is farther from the truth than it is to the standards in which we were met with in life. This, as a fact, is what has caused many of us to have sustained cracks, leaks and major faults in our foundations. And if you topple all of life's events, consequences, turmoil and deposit abuse as part of the equation, you, my friend, may have now been exposed to a foundation with structural or significant damage. Before we go any further, let us define abuse.

Abuse can be described as cruelty, both direct and indirectly applied towards a person or animal of any age for any length or period of time. It can be physical, verbal, mental, emotional and psychological as well. Sadly enough, abuse tends to be cyclic or repeated in nature. This means that, oftentimes, the current victim becomes the victimizer in the future. This stigma could be represented as the infinity symbol that we use today, making it very difficult to determine the end from the beginning.

This notion only motivated me to gain more knowledge on the subject of abuse. After doing some research, I was even more baffled than before. I found some pretty grueling facts that simply knotted my stomach. According to dosomething.org, approximately five children every day die due to child abuse. 1 out of 3 girls and 1 out of 5 boys will be sexually abused before the age of 18. These are still rising at astonishing rates and maybe even larger, due to the fact that many of these crimes go unnoticed and unreported on a daily basis.

Domestic violence too, another form of abuse, is happening at an accelerated and alarming rate as well. Abuse, in any form, has the potential and power to plague anyone with being spiritually blind, deaf or worst-case scenario, feeling spiritually slain. The trademark of abuse is the muting of "outgoing" personalities, nullifying potentiality and the cancellation of primary interest. The person that has been recently subjected to an abusive encounter may literally begin to resemble the outer "likeness" of whom they use to be. They may be reflective of immense sadness and withdrawn.

On the other hand, they may have suddenly become an explosive entity in your home. Tragically, somewhere along an abused person's journey, they may be diverted onto a path that is prone to more abusive and abrasive scenarios as well. This brings me back to the subject and title of this chapter. In bringing the two terms (dilapidated and foundation) together, implies that something was not only broken but mishandled, neglected or ruined from the very beginning. It shows that it is very possible that at our developmental core, the beginning, our circumstances could have already been cracked, damaged or misaligned.

This will ultimately lead to an increased probability of lacking crucial and very fundamental life skills. People that have sustained significant, abusive blows in life tend to lack trust, have trouble distinguishing between love and manipulative situations, maybe sleep impaired, introverted and possess a decreased likelihood of achieving and maintaining success in a timely fashion. However, the key to not only combating but becoming victorious, is in the way that we handle, not ignore, the residue of abuse. In order to react both appropriately and effectively, first, one must be aware that abuse has occurred. As simple as that sounds, in some cases, this may actually take an extended amount of time.

If the individual involved (and under attack) views these actions with a sense of normalcy, abuse will continue to be blanketed by the innocence of ignorance and misguided trust. The abused may actually look at these tragic, mind altering occurrences as being normal and just as dull as partaking in a drink of water. Sadly enough, this lack of emotion, more than likely, did not occur as soon as the abuse started taking place. However, it does mark when numbness has begun to take shape. The person being abused may not even be aware that the venom of abuse is present.

They, more than likely, are unaware that abuse is silently wrapping its grotesque fingers around their necks in an attempt to choke them out, in and throughout life. If abuse has started at an early enough age, chances are, this is the case. For instance, in my case, I was very much so blinded to and by the sexual abuse that I encountered. Being that I started being penetrated at the age of three and it happened on a consistent basis, it was as normal to me as getting up in the morning and brushing my teeth. It was not until I was in elementary school, second grade to be exact, that I had the veils torn from my eyes.

During a police intervention and assembly in the auditorium of Pickett Elementary in Toledo, Ohio I was made aware of the abuse that I experienced on a regular basis. Feeling numb, powerless, eerie and as if I had no other choice at that time, I became fear. Trapped, alone and suffocation would also be quintessential comparisons for me in that splinter in time. With all that I had just learned about "stranger danger," being touched inappropriately and telling an adult about certain situations, immediately altered all that I knew to be true and well. I experienced an amplified sense of shame.

As a child, what was I to do when this was more than an attack on my mind, self-esteem and body? This, and for a very long time, was who I was in totality (or so I thought).

In cases such as these, abuse may actually be fashioned as the "familiar". This can easily translate to abuse feeling both comfortable and correct. But please know that as the abused, it is and was not your fault.

You have done nothing wrong. In fact, it was not you, but your foundation that was in desperate need of repair or total renovation. You are not the identity of what happened to you then, today or even in the days to come. I believe that you are more than a conqueror in the precious and mighty name of Jesus. You shall live and not die.

Because of the battles that you have faced, you are marked by better, wiser and stronger than even you know- right now, today. Please embrace the fact that the world needs you to survive. This has two pertinent and practical meanings. One, we need you here among the living, both physically and spiritually as well. Two, in order for others to move forward, we need you to do your part, as only you can, in the body of Christ.

In addition, we need to know how it is that you were able to make it over the hurdles that continue to hinder and haunt most. We long to hear your testimony of how God equipped you to conquer the strangulation of fear and allowed you to succeed in living a life of abundance, characterized by the flair of freedom in your walk. I long to see you smiling with all that you are, which stems from the core. In order to genuinely accomplish this goal, you must realize that we are not bound by the circumstances that we have faced. You are not called by the conditions that have challenged you.

For example, you do not expect anyone to say to you, "Come here, Molestation" or "Nice to meet you, Neglected." Nor would you expect or answer to, "abused". So why are we still self-mutilating (by the choices that we make and accept) and carrying ourselves as such? We need to break the chains that have us caught in cycles of failure due to distractions and unwarranted distress. In John 8:36, we have learned, if the Son therefore shall make you free, ye shall be free indeed.

So, relinquish fear, doubt and worry as a thing of the past that bids you farewell. Begin living freedom from this moment forward. Imagine yourself as being free to live, free to love and free from the clutter and baggage of your past. We can do this by emptying self and inviting the Holy Spirit in to fill us up until our cup runneth over in His joy, love and strength that is both available and everlasting. Take a moment and a deep, relaxing breath in.

It may assist you to visualize being alone and locked away in a cage. Make the decision and say, "I AM free", aloud. When necessary, repeat it until you feel the atmosphere begin to shift and your burdens lighter. Get up from where you are (mentally), in that cage, and unlatch the door. Walkout.

Make sure to lock the door behind you to prevent your re-entering (knowingly or unknowingly). Continue to take a step forward each and every day without looking back at the lies that detained you in your past. Now pray this prayer over your life:

Prayer

Heavenly Father, I come to you just as I am. Broken, torn and distracted by the things of my past. But Lord, I know with all that I am that you are faithful, loving and knowing of all things pertaining to your child. And yet, You still call me friend. For this, I am blessed beyond all measure and highly above all that I can see. Allow me to view myself as you see me. I ask that you, Father, bless me to trust, seek and abide in you on a daily basis. Make my paths straight and my burdens light. Help me to tread upon waters and remain focused on you. Allow your peace to surpass all of my fears and insecurities as I continue to cast all doubt and worry at your feet. I ask that you bind the hand of the enemy and decapitate my giants right here and now today. For you are my everything and all I have, need and desire is to feel your love and Holy Spirit resting upon me every day of my life. Go out before me and pave the way. I humbly ask that you provide the exit that leads me right back to you. For when the enemy comes in like a flood, the

Spirit of the Lord will (continue to) lift up a standard against him (for me) (Isaiah 59:19). I trust, seek and worship you, my Father, Friend, Comforter, Healer and Redeemer. Your Word is life and I love you.

Amen.

Chapter Three
"The Bottom Of Brokenness"

Jesus said to her, "I am the resurrection and the life. The one who believes in me will live, even though they die; John 11:25

Brokenness is a term that is much too commonplace for comfort these days if you ask me. However, this does not mean that the term is impractical nor is it to be rendered as being untrue. As a matter of fact, brokenness is used to describe fragmented pieces, a separation or violation. And at one point and time, it was the perfected definition of me. It concludes that a crucial piece of the puzzle is "missing," or that something detrimental has taken place that has left its king-sized trenches of void within the confines of the mind, heart and soul.

Brokenness can drastically impair the way a person views him or herself, leaving merely a shadow of self that is no longer esteemed. In addition, the likelihood of maintaining success may seem as if it is barricaded and unattainable. It, in an essence, leaves a warped impression that seemingly stains a vessel, in its entirety. Once someone has continuously collided with misfortune and despairing events, misconceptions, an overwhelming sense of emptiness and an alarming, life sized void are oftentimes the end result. Depression, suicidal thoughts/tendencies, and dancing with darkened life choices are like magnets to this dysfunctional way of thinking.

For those that have never experienced it, brokenness is as vivid and real as the texture of this book. It can be likened to being difficult to see and believe that you are winning when you always feel as though you are the very center of a consistent loss. It dampens even the brightest of days. It somehow allows you to feel as though the darkest shadow not only envelopes but swallows you in totality. Brokenness invades every thought pattern and creates a soaring pessimistic environment that stems from a traumatized and broken heart condition.

Additionally, when a major or systematic violation such as abuse occurs, one not only feels distraught and alone but much like living in a splintered reality saturated with shame. Guilt becomes your first name as unworthiness becomes your shelter. The unhealthy places in which one may seek refuge from the storm maybe in silence, food, sex, self-mutualization, suppression or repression. The participation in ongoing abusive tendencies, is an all too common frequency as well. As a matter of fact, this not only became my vice; it became my zone of comfort.

I can distinctly recall identifying myself as being ruined. I felt a weighted ugliness. I carried this everywhere that I went, like being transfigured by scarring from head to toe, created by a collision, meeting at optimal speeds. The irony in how I was not only feeling but truly believing, was that no one else could see what I was experiencing and harboring within my head and collaborated in my heart. But I, on the other hand, felt its repugnance daily.

When I looked in the mirror, I would just as quickly turn away with a shriek of disgust. I was a freight train, rushing in haphazardly, only to crash and burn on so many different levels and intervals in this life. Abuse, like a heavyweight can opener, had opened up a super-sized portal of self-hate within me. I walked through that portal daily. I hated my huge eyes, dark skin, thin hair, skinny legs and frame, and could go on for days in this fashion.

I considered myself to be drastically negligent of intellect. Permeating the belief that if I had the power to change any one of these things, I would have changed them all and my identity as well, without a second thought. Period. Due to my impeccable ignorance, self-hate and personal experiences, I chose to and loved any and everyone else with an immensity because I could not love myself. Loving myself, according to me then, had proven to be impossible.

I would have outwardly challenged anyone that implied anything contrary to this. I knew with all certainty that I was the very definition of unworthy. This was my truth, clothing and identity daily. I never needed anyone else to remind me. I was the consummation of brokenness.

Thus, I never sought for love to be given unto me in return or as a condition. With the truth being my shield and buckler, my belief system had been warped, shot up and strangled for longer than I could remember. In all actuality, I found these beliefs to be comforting as it led me to expect, receive and entertain everything that I had expected out of people and life. Nothing. Because of this, even as a little girl playing pretend, I was an oddball.

I never did get the rules of playing house quite right. When everyone else wanted to temporarily wear similar characteristics of others, I demanded something totally different. I demanded to be any and everyone else other than myself, every time. This was so much deeper than a little girl's wish. It was my (only) prayer language for extended amounts of time.

I commanded of the Lord to make me someone else, someone worthy, someone lovable. As a result, and to this day, I do not like too much attention or eyes fastened upon me. Hiding from the hurt and being smothered by betrayal, at some point, began to take precedence and a permanent stance in my life. It, inadvertently, altered the person that I was and plagued the choices that I would make. Abuse, seemingly, allows that person to covertly detach themselves.

It dismantles all that you are and single-handedly annihilates your energy level and motivation as well. There were plenty of days that all I wanted to do was sleep. It felt as though the only place that I could find and have a tangible sense of peace was in my dreams. Because I did not have a relationship with nor did I pray unto the Lord, I walked around lost, defeated and harbored a detained spirit as well. Like running on quicksand, my gait, reality and belief systems became disheveled.

I continuously lost my grip on what should (and normally would) matter most. My focus shifted and became as twisted as it was questionable. It could be compared to living in a cloudy world and wearing darkened shades daily. You cannot see the light of day, hope, the world or clearly. If the person that has suffered from abuse is not careful, eventually, it may get to the point that as people try to draw near to them, they may begin to take on the ambiance of evaporation before the world.

Self-isolation may then begin to rear its hideous head. For a long time, this was how I "handled" things, myself and others. If I treated "everything" as if it had no matter of importance, then I could will myself into believing, just that. In turn, things hurt much less. I feared that the motivating principle to anyone being loving towards me was one of corruption and contempt.

I never trusted it or them. So, relaxation or attempting to play it cool was never a viable option for me. Thus, in the end, all that mattered to me was making myself less: vulnerable, transparent, predictable, caring and available (spiritually, emotionally and mentally). This was my protective shielding. I found it to be very effective, although it was fruitless.

I began to put on this persona with such enthusiasm and precision that it became second nature to me. And without realizing it, I actualized a paralyzing numbness pertaining to my feelings. Hence, the creation of new problems and scenarios in my life that stained others as well. There were plenty of times that I knew that I needed to cry in order to secure a sense of relief. However, due to my mishandling of situations, I simply could not cry, show or feel certain bottled up emotions.

This only led to my walking around smiling pretentiously while feeling significantly separated and contradictory to that which was plastered on my face. The most troubling truth pertaining to this scenario was that I found myself struggling to separate the real from the fake, within myself. Never did I realize that I had no recollection of who I really was on any level. It was like seeing myself through an elongated circus mirror. To those of you who know me personally, this will come as a great surprise, but well into my adulthood, I identified myself as and full-heartedly believed that I was cursed.

No if ands or buts about it. It was the totality of who I was. Being that I had experienced sexual abuse on an ongoing basis along with a multitude of other unfortunate events, my self-esteem dwindled (in permanence) below negative. I began to carry this belief to the greatest extent and with all that I was, like a badge of honor. It was etched ambiguously into my choices and traceable in the decisions that I made.

Abuse and its residual were the protagonist of my walk without faith. For me, there was no line of separation in the sand. The abuse that I experienced as a child was like a one-way terminal steering me into the abuse that I chose and suffered from as an adult. It allowed me to believe that the abuse was not only acceptable but also (somehow) very well deserved. But God!

He took me from a place of shattered beyond recognition and the very edge and bottom of brokenness to place characterized by His grace and tender mercies that endure forever and ever. He not only sheltered me from the storm but cradled me in the very palm of His hands. He spoke and the winds of devastation that could have potentially rendered me dead, were silent, still, soothing and transforming. He renewed my mind and spirit. As the Vine, He nourished and revived my soul.

For that, I have no other choice but to rejoice knowing that it (everything that happened in my past) is (current tense) well. Understanding that we (you and I) are all in agreement, that there are times in our lives where we feel broken, defeated and alone. It is at these times that it seems as though we float effortlessly from one devastating circumstance to another situational catastrophe in the making. And just when you begin to believe that things could not get any worse, you begin to plummet to another level much farther beneath the low that originally had us bound. These were the times in my life that I refer to as being at the bottom of brokenness.

When all hope has retreated and life bears only the resemblance of one continuous and brutal beating, can you say that you have experienced the bottom of brokenness? It has a penetrating power that invites all negativity into your personal space. It could be described as the palace of our greatest defeats, the slave quarters in which we succumb to our deepest and darkest fears. It is the wreck-creational room of morbid mentality cages that we are plagued with and accept as undeniable truths. I find hope during these times, imagining that we are like Lazarus.

We have transitioned from illness (our way of thinking) to death (being spiritually slain or caught in an eternal loop of suffering brought about by reliving the abuse). The announcement has been made (by our loved ones). {John 11:3, Lord, the one you love is sick}. We (as the abused) have been considered to be wiped out and cast off emotionally and spiritually. But the Lord, your God has stepped into your present circumstance, condition and cancellation and has defeated your death sentence.

Glory to God! At one time or another, as the abused, we were ill, crippled or defenseless. It may have appeared that the Lord did not move in a timely fashion, on your behalf. As a result of this, a part of us has died and been buried. However, He knows our current situation in great detail.

I believe that He has perfected a time in order to step in and show out as our defense. More than likely, it may have seemed as though we were draped in death (to our sins, beliefs or lack thereof and spirits) before He decided to move days (weeks, months or years) after the fact. Remember, He does not move according to our time frame nor the way that we think. Our Father's movements are coordinated according to His perfect and appointed time, which will inevitably bring about an outpouring of His anointing. Praise God!

He always knows what is best. All that we are required to do is to trust in Him. Keep in mind that Lazarus was dead for four days. I am more than certain that this could have easily seemed like an eternity to Lazarus and those who loved him most. Looking at this in a physical sense, after four days, rigor mortis has more than likely set in and the stench would have had to be unbelievably unshakable.

The dust had settled, and the unanimous decision was in. Lazarus (LaTrice, remove and replace your name here) was dead, which would seem pretty impossible to resolve.

However, these things were intentionally set up and had to happen in order for you to receive your blessing, hear your calling and be met with the purpose that you were created for. In addition, the trials that you were hammered with, glorify our God. It demonstrates how strategic and on time He is.

His perfected timing allows us to be open to receive all that He is offering. Because of it, we now have freedom from all of the things that attempts to ail us and freedom to get up from our current position of defeat, distraction, dismay or any state of sleep. He is commanding us to "Arise." This gives us the ability to come forth (from where we are positioned or hindered) standing on our own feet by His power. As we begin to find our footing, moving step by step, we draw closer to the Trinity (Father, Son and Holy Spirit).

The great part is this, like Lazarus, He still calls us friend.

He spoke and death was erased. Praise God!

Prayer

Heavenly Father, I am in total awe of your beauty. You are awesome in every sense of the word. Lord, you continue to give us beauty for our ashes, strength for our weakness and peace beyond the tears that we cry. I thank you for your faithfulness, love and tender mercies. I thank you for never leaving nor forsaken me, even when you so easily could have. I thank you for holding my hands, being my refuge and the rock of my salvation. Lord, thank you for being with me so that nothing else can stand against me. Allow me to put on your full armor Lord. Please guide, heal and protect me daily. I still struggle even though you have assured me that this battle is not mine but belongs to you. Help my unbelief. Pour out your spirit and cleanse me from the top of my head to the soles of my feet. I belong to you. Yea though I walk through the valley of the shadow of death, I fear no evil for thou art with me (Psalms 23:4). You have turned everything around for my good. Thank you for being here with me in my time of trouble. Thank you for not only answering my cry but for also defeating death for me once again.

Amen.

Chapter Four
"Shattered But Optimistic"

1Samuel 30:18-19
18 And David recovered all that the Amalekites had carried away...
19 And there was nothing lacking to them... David recovered all.

In life, we go through a great many seasons. Some are characterized by beauty and boisterous colors that, in turn, boost and drive our motivation to its maximum capacity. Other seasons, contrarily, tend to be just as void of color as they are cold and fruitless. They become like internal sponges, slowly sucking the very nectar of life out of us, our smiles and our potential to remain proactive in the ongoing pursuit of happiness. With that being said, the majority of people will have no difficulty in believing that "something," an object, can be shattered.

The struggle begins to take form when the declaration is made that someone can, in fact, feel shattered. But in this chapter, my main objective is to show its relevance. I want you to see clearly how someone can view and define themselves as such. Shattered, for me, is best described as broken into unrecognizable shards, shreds or fragmented pieces. It is to describe the extent of something being far greater than damaged.

Shattered, would ultimately declare something as destroyed if it had a voice. It would no longer silence its victims, nor would it make them dangerously loud and violent. Shattered tends to make its victims feel like they are being trapped under unrelenting waters, viewing life through a thick, impenetrable glass. It can single-handedly separate such citizens from society and collapses their chances of achieving the set "norms." It can render its victims as lifeless and weightlessly shifting from one position to the next but never taking any root.

No longer are they limited to simply being affected by the feeling of being shattered. They may inadvertently, actually begin to identify themselves as such. This only enhances their chances to be carried off by the waves of motion (things that they experience) or may render them motionless (reactive not proactive people). The sense of feeling shattered can also easily bear the same resemblance as immobility. This is an actuality and can easily manifest in the spiritual sense but may be demonstrated physically as well.

There are far too many in number, the things that can lead to one feeling shattered, in this lifetime. However, I know one for certain that manages to molest and ravage its victims in totality if appropriate help is not attained. Her name is abuse. She comes in many shades, shapes and forms. My question to you is, does she still live "here" (within you)? Is she still the dictator of your life and corrupter of your choices and potential? When you open your mouth, is she still being heard loud and clear? Or has she simply made your name interchangeable with hers?

These were some of the questions that I was led to ask myself. Over an extended amount of time, I was finally able to answer them honestly. And, yes. She was still very present and ruining my life. With that being said, you may be wondering what the level of difficulty was in asking such questions. The truth of the matter is that it was extremely challenging. I had to actually face me, my fears and a "present" circumstance that threatened to slowly suffocate my ability to achieve healthy relationships and obtain happiness.

In addition, to all of the aforementioned details, I had to be real. For the first time in a very long time, I had to confront a self-centered, head-strong, know-it-all that lacked what mattered most- a relationship with the Lord and a love for self. And as much as I would have loved to, I could not avoid or run from this challenge. What or who could comfort me?

Keep in mind that I was already aware of my every intention, excuse and denial of both parties in me (offense and defensive stances). I could not lie nor could I take a pass. I had to endure like I had to be honest. If I had not, I am almost certain that I would know. In being honest with myself, I had to admit that I was still feeling very chafed to the abuse that I faced as a child.

During this line of self-questioning, I had no other alternative than to face that, head-on. At times it made me feel as though I was standing in front of the firing squad, waiting for someone else to decide whether or not to squeeze on the trigger. Anxious, alone, drained and defeated not only defined but consumed me as well. It was not until much later on in life that I came into the knowledge that I was the death sentence that I faced. I was my own torture chamber. But I still had no clue as to how to refute this inner notion or lack of drive.

Utilizing another analogy, I will attempt to demonstrate how this line of self-questioning can make you feel. I imagine that it could be likened to intentionally attempting to drown yourself, knowing that you can't swim and are terrified of water at every level. Literally, one of the hardest things that you can do, is to look internally for the answers as to why you are continuing to drown in the same shallow waters of your past.

For what seemed like an eternity, I could not progress, although I continued to move forward. I was too busy walking backward in this life, reliving, replaying and rehashing all of the hurt that threatened to cripple me. I was trapped, ruined and discarded while remaining stillness to a fault. This was my result because I was still not seeking shelter in the Father. For this reason, I could not catch my breath, let alone a break if my life depended on it. And it did. Every piece of me, I viewed as tarnished at best which only left me feeling much worse. I was crumpled in totality or so I thought.

At that point in life, the last thing that I wanted to hear in life was the Word of God. But now, I realize that if I had, I would have realized, much sooner, all that I was doing was wrong. In an effort to quickly self-heal, I slowly realized that I was only taking myself through new dimensions of self-hell.

In the Bible, Proverbs 23:7 (KJV), for as a man thinketh in his heart, so is he. And it just so happens that my heart had been constricted and compromised. It was no longer that thing that would go pitter pat or cause me to skip about happily. My heart was comprised of destructive, self-induced tendencies that were constructed by the bed of lies that I was fed and nested upon. Believing those lies, I spoke of them fashionably like hanging gems from collective masterpieces.

I refused to keep them to myself. Whether it was in my voice, body language or my walk, those lies were etched as my permanent truth into all that I did. They became my personal and unfailing belief system. Like being exposed, I was voluntarily, airing my dirty laundry before the world. In doing so, I thought that I was making my life look glamorous and denying the hurt that I still carried heavily in my spirit.

I remember times that I would go out to the club, half naked and not caring because I was showing "me" love. In all actuality, I never truly achieved this goal (loving me) until I was 32 years of age. Yes, having my son at the age of eighteen saved my life. It was the first time that I had experienced such marvelous tenderness's of a phenomenal love, unsullied. I devoured every moment and excitedly craved more. But the truth of the matter was that I was still lost.

My question to you is simple. How many of you know that God uses what we view as a "loss" and miraculously spins it into victory? He recognizes the problems that we face and even the ones that we may have caused and still manages to love and bless us beyond our wildest beliefs and contempt. He not only can but will pick up the jagged pieces of life that threaten to splinter and damage the way that we see ourselves.

Even when we feel shredded into bits, know that He is aware and concerned for us. God has a way of putting the pieces back into place so tenderly that we have no other alternative than to come out better than we were before. We stand only to gain in His presence. We attain wisdom, strength, increased faith and patience.

Additionally, we become more heavily dependent on our Father, Strong-tower, Master and Savior. Praise God!

He can take adversity and rotate it into virtuosity. May I mention, within the blink of an eye. I know because He has done it a great many times on my behalf. In the Word, it teaches us that, in our time of need, He will intercede for us. According to John 14:16 (KJV), and I will pray the Father, and he shall give you another Comforter, that he may abide with you forever.

How promising is that? Even when we feel as though we have experienced a crippling defeat at the hands of our enemies, abusers or even if self-stimulated, God still allows us to recover all that was lost and more. All that we have to do is confess, believe and call upon the name of the Lord. Hallelujah.

Over time, I have found that the promise in John 14:16 for a "Comforter" is the Word of God. It encourages, produces life, strengthens, instructs and gives us warnings as well. The Word of God speaks. But my question directed towards you is, are you focused, listening and inviting the Holy Spirit in?

If so, there is hope accompanied with gain and sustenance. The Word is as alive as it is nourishing. Even in my most severe state of feeling shattered, I found and felt resurrection. Instead of choosing to coexist with and in the dark, I absorbed and experienced the light (radiance and lessened burdens). By diving in and meditating on the Word of God, I inadvertently sought and secured shelter in my King.

You will find that no matter what issue you are currently facing, the Bible has a liberating occurrence compatible with yours. When feeling shattered, ruined and victimized, I implore you to read 1Samuel 30:1-20. You will find it not only to be a rewarding read but also applicable to you and your situation as well. It gives you a voice to speak to and command the mountain that you are faced with to move right now.

In this delicious chapter in the Old Testament, David is faced with imminent defeat. He and his soldiers have returned home (a place that you would expect to experience safety and security) and found it on fire (which equates to destruction or a state of ruin). The women and children had been abducted (the love was gone). In verse four, it said that David and his men wept until there was nothing left. How many times have we cried ourselves to sleep because of the issues staining or hardening our hearts?

Well, the great news is that this is not the end of the story. David's people wanted to stone him because they blamed him for giving the original orders for them to leave their families. How many times have your closest loved ones turned on and wanted to harm you during your storm?

I have read multiple translations and have concluded that David did not feel comforted in knowing that everyone taken captive was still alive. Some may challenge this belief, but I felt convicted by the Holy Spirit as I read over this passage. It was if he was confirming that there are worse things than being dead. Some of us have experienced and survived those things: rape, abuse or enslavement. Praise God.

My next question to you is, how many of us are still being enslaved by the molestations of our past? How many of us have returned home and found a fire that was raging and staring back at us? Even if this describes your current circumstance and dilemma, we, like David, can encourage ourselves in the Lord. David went to the Lord, asking, seeking and knocking. Reassured that God was the **only** answer, he waited, listened and took appropriate actions according to his faith. We should do the same.

No matter the circumstance, even if it looks like a capitalized defeat, God will supply an exit. But, have you positioned yourself to receive it? In David's case, the Lord allowed his men to find an Egyptian that was left for dead. The soldiers brought him to David. In a time of war, most would have decapitated their enemies, especially ones that admitted to helping to capture their family members; however, this was not the fate of this Egyptian.

When your master (the parent or man responsible for you) had left you for dead, your Master (God) will bring about healing. Like the Egyptian, God will send someone to clean your wounds, feed you, help to quench your thirst and supply you with delicacies. In return for doing the "peculiar" thing at a time of war, the Egyptian blessed David to find his enemies that were in a drunken (vulnerable and sleeping) state. The Amalekites were much larger in number but easily defeated due to being drunk and scattered about in various lands. All of this, of course, was in God's hands.

In addition to being made victorious, receiving everything he lost, David also received the spoils (belongings) from the Israelite and Philistine towns that were also raided. Each translation highlighted the fact that David was missing nothing. Praise God. Nor will you. Whatever is ailing you, prevents you from resting, or securing peace, give it to God. He will heal you from the top of your head to the soles of your feet. When He touches you, you will never be the same. He is your restoration, waiting to happen. He will leave you wanting for and missing nothing.

Prayer

Heavenly Father, I come to you in thanksgiving of all that you are to me. You are my everything. Lord, I need you right here and now. Please speak to my heart. I long to hear from you. I want to know your perfect will for my life Lord. You are invited in. Have your way, Lord. Touch me as only you can. Give me your peace that surpasses all understanding and forgive my sins. Allow me to trust in you like never before. Lord, I humbly ask that you make a way out of no way. Part the red sea for me, Father. Make what was meant for my bad to now be used for my good. You are awesome, just and sovereign in all your ways. I thank you for your faithfulness and for not allowing any weapons to prosper pertaining to me. Lord, I ask that you allow me to experience your freedom. John 8:36 (KJV): If the Son, therefore, shall make you free, ye shall be free indeed. I declare and decree freedom in Jesus name.

Amen.

Chapter Five

"Searching and Finding Devastation"

Numbers 15:39

You will have these tassels to look at and so you will remember all the commands of the Lord, that you may obey them and not prostitute yourselves by chasing after the lusts of your own hearts and eyes.

In life, I believe that at some point, we have all been searching. As a matter of fact, some of the searches that we have invested in may have been abstract and obsolete. On the other hand, others were boisterous, charismatic and dripping with clarity. Those searches may have stemmed from those things deemed as trivial to those marked by magnificence. Either way, the searches that we have initiated inwardly will somehow effortlessly manifest outwardly, with or without our permission.

So, my question to you is, what are you looking for? Secondly, do you know what will be required in order to quench or alleviate your thirst? Are you aware, or are you still oblivious as to where this "need", or "void" has originated from? Most importantly, will this "needed" addition, bless you with "life" (sustenance) or will it detach and drain you to the point of death?

Prior to taking any actions, we must acknowledge the fact that there is no way for us to ascertain this without going to our loving Heavenly Father. I implore you to activate your faith by applying this notion as your very first step. Before making any drastic or sudden moves, position yourself in an active and ongoing prayer life.

This is your shelter in any of the storms that you face. It is equivalent to advancing upward and utilizing your power to move over a muted and defenseless enemy. In doing so, not only does this make it mandatory for us to speak, but it allows your request to be known unto the Lord. In addition, it is just as essential for us to wait and then listen for His voice. In doing so, it offers Him an invitation to be the director of our path.

Without doing this, we are broken before we begin. We then leave no other alternative for ourselves then to respond in direct opposition (at times) to His promises towards us. Remember, His promises are forever, Yes and Amen. However, we can oftentimes, somehow twist and finagle our ways to the point that we are seemingly plagued as victims. Instead of being set free and living a life of abundance in a victorious yet silenced fashion, we begin to live bound, broke and complacent.

The sad part is this; some of us are (unknowingly) still dancing to a tune that no one else can see, hear or feel. Unbeknownst, this fruitless dance only furnishes us with much wasted time and energy spent. So my question to you would be, what exactly is the point of this great show (the guessing games that we play) which harvests no return or chance to recover anything positive on your investments (ideas, time and energy that you have buried)? This dance, I will now entitle as pretense, as it sometimes will single-handedly, pervert the truth in one way or another. As a matter of fact, this dance in life has the capability and potential to fool even the master pretender.

It isn't until we attempt to mask or ignore the hurt that we have carried for so long, that it will find a way to erupt. Like living life on the edge of danger, pretense explodes onto a surface in life that will cause the most crippling damage and is least expected or contained. This damage comes in a variety of forms, including fear, anxiety, unforgiveness, hatred, intoxication, and addiction, just to name a few. Not only does it ruin self, but it also cleverly transfers onto others that are close in approximation as well.

Matthew 6:33 commands us to seek ye first (not last nor will second be good enough) the kingdom of God, His righteousness, and all things (of Him- fruits of the spirit, wisdom, grace and things of the like) shall be added unto you. If we are not aligning ourselves in accordance to this Biblical principle and practice, we effortlessly ensnare ourselves. We then become unaware of the blatant differences between what is real and what is obviously false. This is contrary to the character created and intended for the edification of Christ that resides within us. Not only will this lead to morbid blindness, it also staples defeat to our backsides. Not seeking God first, could be likened to choosing darkness as your veil and then complaining that you cannot see; it could just as easily be identified as setting a trap for your worst enemy, and then frantically falling prey to it yourself.

I know that this thought may be hard to digest. However, if the truth were told, this analogy is both symbolic of and submerged in truth. The indisputable fact is that sometimes we are our own worst enemy. Both intentionally or unintentionally alike, we can seamlessly fall victim to our own schemes, devices and worst fears.

In some cases, this is our recurring role in life (falling or failing at every angle). It is as if we have placed emphasis on repeat and prance about proudly as if stopping the broken cycle is not the valid, viable or available option. With this sort of mentality, we continue to beat ourselves down, directly and indirectly and fail to be recharged, refreshed and renewed in Christ by remaining prayed up. Spiritually, we begin to look like the fool trying to win the one-man, one-legged marathon. We fight the war against no one (not the enemy) but position ourselves to pulverize the opponent labeled as self. And we succeed, not win, whenever we invest in the wrong search missions.

After we have worn ourselves out in every sense imaginable, we then place the blame on any and everyone else, as if God has not tried to warn us or provide an exit strategy. Please be advised, that a) your listening ears must be not only on but tuned in as well to hear what the Holy Spirit is saying. B) your heart must be right (soft, receptive, repentive and responsive), in order for you to receive and comprehend a word from the Lord. Keeping in mind that He may just be speaking to you right now. Are you listening?

Recognizing the wiles of the enemy immediately or even better, beforehand, is a way that we can ensue victory and come out better than we were before. Realize that "this" strategy (the attack that you are currently under) generally begins with the mindset. Look at it this way. If you believe it (self-imposed or enemy generated), good or bad, you can and will achieve it. Therefore, these attacks are like customized battlefields aimed at hitting you in a blind or unprotected area.

In an effort to cripple and detain you, the enemy will stop at nothing. The greater your potential, whether you believe in it or not, the greater he will fight against both of you (person and purpose). If the enemy has started adamantly warring against you, as early as shortly after your birth, you are housing greatness within. For this reason, he will continue to hand feed you lies that may seem consistent to "your" truth. Lies that cause you great grief and leave you feeling unloved, unworthy and not wanting to participate any further in this life are of him, not of you and most certainly are not true!

These lies are snares from a fowler that aims to prevent you from progressing and believing that we can and will be met with our God-given purpose, a life of abundance and endless joy. And if he cannot stop you, then he will attempt to drain you spiritually, mentally and physically. To him, this is just as good. If he can keep you distracted by having you look in all the wrong directions, ineffective by sitting on an endless standby and maintain your identity as a consistent fruitless entity, he has won.

But I am here to implore you to no longer stand silently in agreement with this untruth. My job now and always is to make sure that you are aware that even if it appears that he has a one to zero lead, you are to keep pressing. Keep advancing anyhow. While he has what is temporary and the "appearance" of ownership, it is not his to possess. You have an eternal victory (beginning right here and right now) with your name on it. Your best victory yet is awaiting your "true" arrival with destiny. Wake up, get in and equipped through Christ Jesus!

Even though you may be tired to the point of exhaustion, all that is required of you is that you be in possession of a minuet faith. Allow that faith to be loud enough to give you the audacity to declare the Word over your life. Then speak to "that" mountain and command it to move. In doing so, we must specifically call "that" mountain by name. No matter the size or name (self-hatred, fear, poverty, unbelief, addiction, gender confusion, unforgiveness) of your mountain, command it to move, be canceled or uncreated in Jesus mighty and precious name. Afterward, you can breathe with a sigh of relief, begin to taste the recompense of freedom and move forward from the pit that once cradled you. Glory to God.

I know, all too well, both sides of this pilgrimage (Searching for peace, love, God (verbally) while still unconvinced of His love, mercy and faithfulness towards us. This too, was a part of my very own journey. And, I will admit that yes, sometimes it takes more time than we are willing to invest in our development to take place. But no matter what you do, keep trusting, believing God, fasting and praying until the change takes place in your heart first (spiritual) prior to it than being made manifest in the physical realm.

In the interim, God endows us with a thorn in our side or even a limp. This is something that He has blessed us with as a reminder of the struggle that we faced and would not have overcome without Him intervening. We then turn to the thorn in our side (that we were blessed to possess) and begin to place blame and focus on its contents. Rather than allowing God to use it to stretch and develop us further, we utilize it as the root of our rebellious tendencies to mask the hurt that we feel. We then (as the abused) find ourselves searching for crutches to comfort instead of crying out to God to prevent, prevail and permeate the atmosphere that we face or reside in.

This internal battle that we are facing on our own promotes us to believe that we can "become the prevention" of a hardened or broken heart. We then follow up by creating grave sites (a place where nothing can live, grow or bloom) in or along with our hearts. Next, we construct shallow walls that easily cave, or self-implode anyhow. This will only lead to a road of self-battery and assault if we are not careful and cognizant.

Inadvertently, or so it may seem, this is exactly how some of us have (in the past) or are (currently) treating ourselves daily. Like raging civil war within ourselves, which is a battle that can never truly be won. We just keep grabbing for those things that will continue to cause us harm. Although I wanted and needed to quit the self-inflicted abuse and cycles of destructive tendencies, I could not. At that time and still today, I wondered, why had I become so numb? Could it be that I had become so desensitized, due to the abuse that I faced, that I was no longer aware of the actions and the consequences thereof?

Well, my ugly truth is that I knew but cared not. I believed, at that time, that I deserved every bad thing that happened in my life, which is contrary to the Word of God. Showcasing this faulty belief system, I flung the doors wide open. I invited them all in by name. My actions spoke, "Come on in despair, depression, betrayal, lack and frustration, you are one of my favorites!" Many other atrocities had invitations and trudged in as well. While my mouth continued to proclaim self-love, my actions continued to denounce every bit that it heard.

This is what can happen over time when you have experienced abuse. You continue to look for love in all the wrong places. You then refuse to place God in the only unoccupied space left available and in dire need of Him-your heart. Often times and in response to the trauma experienced, we begin to not only expect but to accept the inexcusable. We can become unloving, manipulative, hard to read, unapproachable, oversensitive and untrusting of others. In this book, I encourage you to redesign your search and it will, in turn, redesign you.

Psalms 121:1, I find to be of great encouragement. It says, I will lift up my eyes (change your viewpoint. Look up, above your current "status," towards God) unto the hills from whence cometh my help. Your help cometh from above: which means that He will exceed your expectations when you become heavily dependent upon Him. Allow this idea to motivate you to do three things: wake up, seek the Light and speak the hardcore truth daily. This will bring about fervent freedom that is not easily converted or distracted from.

In order to wake up, one must first acknowledge and see all circumstances for what they are or are not. And more specifically, we can no longer participate as viewing things as we would like them to be. Sometimes this is as painful as colliding with a blunt force object. But there is still good news. Negativity, hardships, and defeat were labels addressing your past. You have the power, authority and choice to move on from there. Like the changing of an address, you can change the climate of your atmosphere as well.

Secondly, you can choose to seek and pursue the Light. By looking for the positive in every situation, we refute what we see. Agreeing that what we see with our physical eyes is temporary, we become equipped to carry irrefutable, uncontainable and irreversible faith in what we believe God for. When we shift our focus from man, our situations and ourselves, we invite the Holy Spirit in to have His way.

It is here that we surrender from self and pilgrimage toward an ever faithful, all-knowing God that cares for us immensely. It is at this time that we fasten our gaze upon the hills which cometh our help and not the turmoil that we face. If we then fix our focus long and hard enough, we will be able to detect the very slightest move of God taking place on our behalf. It's like saying, "Ok, God. Here I am, in the ring, boxing gloves on, with my hands dangling comfortably at my side. For this battle is no longer mine but yours. And you win every time."

Inviting the Way, Truth and The Light in, will cancel the darkness that once cocooned our joy, potential and prosperity. Actively partaking in these actions shall indeed annihilate the darkness that traps, intimidates and suffocates us silently. In order to experience bold and heartfelt freedom, one must ask, seek, knock and await the **only** answer to our prayers. We must be not only open but inviting of the Holy Spirit. We must accept the fact that we do not know everything, nor can we do anything without Him, but fail.

With this being said, I believe that most people will contemplate whether or not the premeditated plan will be beneficial to them. We tend to think about the advantages versus disadvantages scale. This view will only limit us to seeing things in the physical and present tense, which is like inviting a false positive into the equation. Although this appears to be a good beginning, it is not the best method to utilize.

This too, is an example of utilizing the wrong search engine. Practices such as these only create a brilliant blind spot on the monitor that we are so heavily reliant upon (us and what we believe that we know). Please be advised that no matter the current rate of speed at which we travel along this journey or how cautious we intend to be, we are in grave danger if this is the action plan that we employ or invest in. Due to our ignorance and the magnificent blind spot on our radar, we are unable to lay eyes upon or even detect the fast-approaching enemy. Like unknowingly opening ourselves up for failure and ruin, we then engage in unannounced spiritual games of Russian Roulette. That now hidden object, is aimed at wrecking or colliding with us. The question is, will you be blindsided or prepared?

Unequipped and unable to handle the magnitude of the fallout is what we will be if we are not aligning ourselves with God in consistent prayer. Depending on ourselves, invites us to experience a premature fulfillment without knowledge or evidence of the void that it may also be creating simultaneously. Applying this technique may inadvertently lead you down a dark winding path of deception. Equipped with the wisdom that all things take place in the spiritual realm prior to being met with in the physical is key. We must seek guidance and preparation from the grandeur posture realized through prayer.

If you gain nothing else from this chapter, hold tight to this. We need to seek the Lord first and diligently (constantly). While remaining vigilant at all times, we must forever fasten His praises upon our lips. I encourage you to dig deep within yourself and ask the questions aforementioned in this chapter. Remember, total honesty and surrender leads to total victory. Keeping in mind that we are in a constant battle of the mindset, we have no more allotted time for guessing games, distractions or succumbing to anything less than God's very best for our lives.

Question. Can you ever remember a time when you gave your all searching for and actually achieving a goal based and focused on what you just had to have? And once you received it, took it home, polished it up and put your name on it, it cost you the most excruciating pain or embarrassment? Well, let me tell you something. You don't have to experience this if you haven't. I have done it enough for the both of us. This thing that I had experienced and just had to have was called a relationship. One without God as the administrator and guide. As a matter of fact, the Holy Spirit (that I had no relationship with at the time) continued to tell me no. And I aggressively continued to lunge forward in, yes. Huge mistake. It always leads to deception created by and inflicted upon self.

If you are not certain what it means to accept His best for your life, research the scriptures for yourself. This equips you to speak life, declare healing, walk into freedom, proclaim victory and experience the fullness of joy. While others continue searching endlessly for self, love, acceptance, peace, the meaning of life or prosperity, you can now stop. He **is** the answer and our source. He is our foundation and our portion. Once again, He calls you and I, friend. Praise God!

Will you accept Him, or will you continue to turn away in the captivation of falsified searches and malignant finds? I challenge you to redefine your search. I simply ask you this rhetorical question. What do you have to look at daily that serves as a reminder of the faithfulness, omnipresence and commands of the Lord? What do you possess that will prevent you from prostituting (sullying or polluting) yourself by chasing after your own desires and not His?

Do not modify, drastically change the way that you search for meaning. Change it from looking for mundane and unattainable (without Him). Because without the greatest sacrifice ever made, Jesus, we search only to find devastation, rejection, confusion or get involved in events that leave us feeling as if we are submerged in guilt. Begin looking with great expectation, to accept and realize the BEST gift that costs us nothing to receive and Him everything to give- salvation, grace and mercies everlasting.

Prayer

Heavenly Father, I come to you once again in total surrender, knowing that I am in great need of you right here and now, Lord. I accept that your word is true and pertains to me in totality. In you, I am free, loved and well cared for. I thank you for being the good Shepherd that will leave the flock to come upon the one that is lost, hurt

and defenseless. That sheep is me. Thank you for meeting me here Father. I thank you that your love has no limits nor comparison and covers a multitude of sin. Cover me, Lord. Strengthen me where I am weak and remove every trace of anything that is not of you. Lord, bless me to seek you diligently as I know that you a rewarder to those that do. I thank you that in your Word, it says that I should not be afraid of the terror by night nor the arrow that flieth by day. You are my strong tower. Therefore, destruction has missed me every time because of my faith in You. I surrender as I repent for anything that is not pleasing in your sight Lord. I ask all of these things in the name of the Father, Son and Holy Spirit.
Amen.

Chapter Six
"ASK"

Read: Luke 11. Focusing on vs 5-10

Once again, I have to thank my Heavenly Father for His strategic placement, guidance and innovative instruction in my life. In accordance to His perfect will and timing, He continuously makes intercession for us. With that being said, I am more than certain that we all, for the most part, can agree that the Lord has a magnificent yet settle way of ordering even the simplest of our steps. Whether we are totally obedient or not, the Lord consistently makes sure that we hear the very specific words that we need to hear at the time that we need to hear them the most. In times that our spiritual nourishment is dwindling to the point of delinquency, He will move mountains, break chains and shift the atmosphere in order to gain our fullest attention.

All that we are required to do is be willing to receive Him and ask. God has continued to be very deliberate when ensuring that we learn a great many things, including but not limited to the fact that He is forever present and very much so real. He is always in the current state of working things out in such a fashion that cancels any doubt of His everlasting love towards us, nor does it neglect to magnify Him as the Author and Finisher of our Faith. He also goes to great lengths to prove that His authority and power, Praise God, are endless. Therefore, I will choreograph this chapter in an attempt to deliver the message in the same manner that it was given to me.

As of September 17, 2018, I began to truly realize that my every step had indeed been ordered. Between the months of March through May, I experienced the very worst months of my life. But in all actuality, right in the midst of my wilderness experience, I was able to feel His presence permeating and closely. Feeling Him, as I cried out, turned out to be one of my greatest blessings. This allowed my closed mind to be rendered more effective as my spiritual eyes were made manifest (or open).

Even when it appeared that I was "invisible" at the new church that I attended, He never forgot about, failed or for a moment allowed me to believe that I had been forsaken. As I bowed down to pray and surrender my all to Him, I remember, literally, being rocked ever so delicately, like a newborn baby in a crib. At times, as my eyes filled with tears, a sweet aroma would then fill the space that I was in. In these moments, all that I could do was begin to praise Him. Hallelujah. Right there in the midst of the storm threatening to ruin you, I encourage you to praise Him. This helps to shift the atmosphere on our behalf, leaves room for Him to move in as it causes confusion. It also decapitates the head of our enemy. Thus, praising Him becomes like a warm blanket fresh out of the dryer; it not only covers, it empowers us. Praise God.

Before having these close encounters with Him in 2018, I mirrored the feelings that I buried and found shelter in. Constantly feeling much less than loved and colored as the antithesis of worthy, I became the perfect definition of being draped in despair due to the crippling circumstances that I faced with a multitude of people, alone. It seemed as though everything that I knew, loved and trusted was lost and irretrievable. As the feeling of abandonment intensified, the bitterness that I experienced was colder than any winter that I have ever known. I remember wearing a weariness that consumed me to the point of brittleness. And yet, the Lord (when you allow your perspective to shift, you'll realize this too) gave *me* (fill your name in here) the strength to endure. I persisted in silence (you have to be careful who you share things with) more often times than not, but I committed to progress forward. I remained obedient to what I knew to be an unfading and impeccable truth. I remember continuing to press my way forward to the women's Bible study at Calvary Chapel in Newport News, Virginia, faithfully.

Hearing those women (that were strangers to me at the time) speaking life so powerfully and eloquently, altered my life. The Word cleansed, pierced and stirred my soul. My abbreviated way of thinking changed radically in such a short period of time that I am still shocked to this day. Their influence which, was the direct reflection of the love of God residing within them and the atmosphere that was generated thereof, in an hour and a half (week after week), allowed me to not only hold on but cling tightly unto the Lord, my God. I began to crave with my whole being, what they had. It seemed that each woman that had the privilege of speaking to the group possessed a tangible (or so it seemed) power from on high. They elevated, educated and endowed His children to walk upright spiritually, no longer slumped over by the weight of sin, unforgiveness or shame.

They gave unselfishly, each week. Those women of God purged and denied themselves in order to pour out His Spirit unto a thirsty generation through His word. I will forever be grateful. This type of profound power cannot be found or tapped into in every environment that we encompass. Therefore, I cherish both it and them. They spoke and the broken, contrite spirit residing within fell off as the Holy Spirit began to rise up. I felt a separation taking place that was both liberating and divine. My mind shifted from a position of trying to dictate, facilitate and orchestrate the move of God to having a heart of worship that allowed me to humbly ask, seek and wait patiently upon the Lord.

When the Holy Spirit enters in and has control, there should be some sort of sign. All of my life, up to this point, I had lived as a lamb. Nevertheless, being planted firmly in the Word, I begin to evolve as a lion. The Word is alive. It comforted me to the point of resembling the caressing touch of a loved one. The Word dried my tears and protected me as the Sword that it was created to be. The Word of God altered my life to such a degree that it allowed me to see the shattering of the untruth that I had previously bid as infallible to now be rendered as being just as fragile as it was false.

Many of you may be wondering how this was made possible. Well, it is very simple. I began to thirst for the power, protection, transformation, and wisdom found only in the Living Word of God. You see, it is never enough to simply hear (being preached at) the Word. We have to speak (cover ourselves like soap with) and walk (think, act and move in accordance) with the Word. This will bring Light to dark and rotting places that attempt to remain concealed from everyone, including the person that it attaches itself to.

In doing so, freedom and transformation was formed. I remember pleading with the Lord to allow me to be able to speak with specific leaders and thank them for allowing themselves to be used as a conduit that continuously poured out His Spirit upon me. In a time covered by darkness so harsh that it would have easily canceled kindness and compassion time and time again, they spoke, and the enemy's plans were effortlessly dismantled.

The words freely forming at their lips were like heavy duty shovels, digging deep within and uprooting false beliefs, realities and practices. The women then began to fill those places of void with God's incorruptible, undeniable Word of truth. In due time, I experienced His joy (believe it or not, this is a choice that we can make no matter the time or temperature of our circumstances), as I continued to go through the fire. Just as quickly, or so it would seem, I was able to speak with, thank and get connected to those in leadership that had greatly impacted my life. Praise God.

By the middle of September 2018, I was in the process of being mentored by the same women of God that had been such a great blessing and inspiration to me. We, as the women's ministry had been reading and working out of a very powerful workbook (and must read) entitled, *Lord, I Give You My Heart* by Bobbie Hawkins and Teresa Shaw. Investing quality (uninterrupted) time with Him in order to complete the homework assignments and gain a better understanding has an undeniable, "unlocking" mechanism attached. Spending time, intentionally with Him, with no ulterior motive, prompted much growth, stimulated change, created courage, decalcified my heart and liberated my soul.

As a matter of fact, in a dream that I had in June of that same year, the Holy Spirit showed me that I would be speaking to the women that gathered for the women's Bible study. For me, the dream served as confirmation of multiple things. First of all, it showed me who I was or would become. Secondly, it, or so I thought, told me that I would be able to speak to the women during that session during Bible study.

To say that I was elated would be an understatement. I felt that this was only a small part of His process in order for my purpose to be fulfilled and met with my passion. In having this vision, I was encouraged to invest even more time, focus and energy than I ever had in my Bible. Using my Bible as a source to cross reference the information found on the pages of that book, was fundamental and the basis to attaining spiritual growth and development.

I began to research names, parables, family history, origin, and geography. I began to ask how "this" passage pertained to me. Fully exonerated by the belief that nothing is coincidentally placed in the Bible, allowed the people, places and experiences to not only take on life but, in some cases, prove pertinent to my current state of being. This is what is meant by receiving a Rhema word. As I combed through the pages of my Bible and answered the questions posed in the workbook, I could not help but hear my name being called. I became beyond determination to remember key verses. As I read of Him and His ways, He read me, but did not stop there. He then showed me my heart as I raised it up towards Him to cleanse, heal, protect and revive the darkened areas to a renewed state of better than before.

How many of you know that when you are made vulnerable (lay out prostrate {in totality and honesty} before the King) and expose the bruises and callouses of your heart in total surrender, God has a way of getting directly to the root of what is ailing you. As He begins the cleansing process, He begins speaking to you in a perfectly plain fashion. In doing so, the Holy Spirit will give you new revelations pertaining to that old festering wound that many of us have been harboring for years. He will show you how that "thing" (abuse, betrayal, neglect, hate) began to weep (leak, spill over) onto every area pertaining to you. He will then patiently begin to reveal to you, how "it" was used as a vehicle to corrupt your character, way of thinking, behavior and perception.

This is exactly where the Lord gains your focus, faith and trust. As He continues to gently mold, renew and transform you, your resurrection takes place as elevation takes hold. Psalms 23:4, Yea, though I walk through the valley of the shadow of death (places, events and situations that look like they will indeed cause our demise), I will fear no evil for thou art with me. I always like to add, holding our hands, making a way where there appears to be none and providing a timely exit, which guarantees our success in and through Him.

By the time that I received the assignment to do a 10-minute reflection for October 22, 2018, in the chapter titled, Persevering, I felt like I was ready and well prepared. I began reading Luke 11:5-13, several times a day, like my life depended on its impartation. I began seeking a new word or revelation from an old and familiar scripture, like an investigative detective hunting pertinent forensic evidence to solve a case. Not only did this Bible study feel nourishing, but it also highlighted grave areas in my life and way of thinking that were in great need of powerful prayer that would, in turn, facilitate a radical change.

How many of you know that the Lord will give you (allowing you to see, taste or feel for) an assignment, the desire of your heart or a fulfillment of a promise at His appointed time, not yours? Sometimes, the Lord will give us a vision without an activation, expiration date, or cancellation notice and permit these things to come to pass according to His perfected will for our lives. And then there are times that we are ready mentally (us), but spiritually (in Him) are not ready or positioned in preparedness to fulfill the maximum level of efficacy for someone else's time of need.

I make mention of these specific ideas in order to send a notice. Sometimes when we have seemingly been placed on pause, it should stand as a reminder that "it" (everything that we experience) is not about us. Everything has to be about, centered around and focused on Him. When we invite the Holy Spirit in to direct our path, we (as believers) will not be put to shame (Romans 10:11).

Be mindful that, more often times than not, things do not work out as we have planned. For this reason, we should remain thankful, positive and prayerful. Trust the Lord, your God, in totality (which is NOT always easy). Secondly, we must learn to wait with patience for His appointed time, which always proves to be far more superior to our way of thinking.

Remember, God is not a man, that He should lie; neither the son of man, that He should repent (Numbers 23:19). His Word and the vision that He gave you will come to pass in due season. But while you are waiting, simply be so inclined to ask the questions etched on and troubling your heart. In addition, always remember to pray genuinely, "Father, not my will but your will be done" (Luke 22:24). Sometimes we have to remain seated (vigilant, steadfast in the Lord, grounded in the Word of God and prayed up) prior to being put to into a position that demonstrates His power.

And it is in the power of the Holy Spirit, that we experience an unabbreviated love. He said unto me, "Like a flower, we must first be potted (placed to the point of being held down) in nutrient rich soil." In terms of defining the richness of the soil, one must equate that the darker the appearance of what has surrounded the plant (us), the better. The darkness that we have been planted in a) promotes growth and will b) inevitably lead to the Light if we believe and seek ye first the Kingdom of God (Matthew 6:33).

The darker your situation appears to be, the greater potential you will possess (period). We have to be placed in the perfect atmosphere (which differs for each and every one of us) that will promote our personal and spiritual growth. We are then watered (which transports the proper nutrients throughout the plant, cells and roots as well as to help it (us) to stand). The term watering is referring to the Word of God. Afterward or during this time, we must be arranged in either direct (hearing from the Holy Spirit) or indirect (the preaching of the word or confirmation from someone else) Son light. This process ensures that the plant (us) will grow and have the energy needed to continue to thrive.

As we wait patiently on the Lord, we can then begin to praise Him in advance. Ask Him to remove flesh (selfish nature and tendencies) so that we may be blessed enough to receive Him (His will and not our way). Thus, when we feel most charged up and set on "go," we are in an ideal position to reevaluate the contents and desires of our hearts. Ask yourself, who are you promoting first and foremost? If it is not Him, pause, pray and then proceed.

Secondly, we should ask, "Who is in charge?" When we finally realize that it is not us, it will only be that much easier to grab and hold onto silence. Take a seat and wait to be chosen for His perfected time to complete the task at hand. This should be in accordance with His view (which is both monolithic and perfected versus our view, which is minuscule and defective).

Now, in realizing that, I began to comprehend this: It was not in His design for me to speak at that time in revelation to this which He has given me. If I did that (talking out of turn) then, I would not be doing this (writing His book) now. The Lord's plans for my life may still be for me to speak directly (in that place) or indirectly (through this book) to those women. However, I must ask, seek, knock and wait for His answer.

His plans are always (no matter how it feels) what is best for us. If we are obedient and hold on to His promises, He will, on every occasion, exceed our expectations. My plans were to speak (momentary) to them. His command was to write (legendary, which transcends my time here on earth) in order to reach a greater (numerical) audience. Prior to this, He had to speak to, cleanse and transform my heart so that I could hear Him more clearly and follow suit. Glory to God!

I will begin as I am led to, with Luke Chapter 11, verses 5 through10 (NKJV). And it reads, And He said to them, "Which of you shall have a friend, and go to him at midnight and say to him, 'Friend, lend me three loaves; for a friend of mine has come to me on his journey, and I have nothing to set before him'; and he will answer from within and say, 'Do not trouble me; the door is now shut, and my children are with me in bed; I cannot rise and give to you'? I say to you, though he will not rise and give to him because he is his friend, yet because of his persistence he will rise and give him as many as he needs. "So, I say to you, ask, and it will be given to you; seek, and you will find; knock, and it will be opened to you. For everyone who asks receives, and he who seeks finds, and to him who knocks it will be opened.

While reading verse five, I heard the Holy Spirit say, "pause, you need to recognize the difference between Friend (Him), and friend as the same difference between covenant and contract. In Christ Jesus, we have the confidence in knowing that there is no greater love ever shown or directed towards us. God is the only one that is and will always be there whenever and wherever we call. We love Him because He first demonstrated His everlasting love towards us. It was not based on the conditions that we are faced with, the place that we were found (in sin) or even what we could bring to the table. Our unity with our Friend was built upon His love, purity, gentleness and His ultimate sacrifice. His love created our relationship and it cost Him his life. He gladly exchanged His life in order to put on our sin. That love continues to redeem us to this day. Christ, as our Friend is a covenant, which means our bond or relationship is eternal (everlasting) and unilaterally (stemming from one {Him} as our source) based.

Contrarily, the friends that we make here on earth, nowadays, could be likened to having contractual (bilateral or requiring of two) agreements. As long as you are beneficial to me, and I am to you, we are in a committed relationship. The very moment that this changes, we as being friends (partners, spouses) are typically concluded as we begin moving to separate but greener geographical locations. We are then (by calling people friend) simply handing out titles to those who: do not show us a genuine, selfless love; may intentionally cause us harm or unassign/neglect responsibilities when we are in need.

This is a total contradiction to His plans for us. Jeremiah 29:11 (NIV), For I know the plans I have for you," declares the Lord, "plans to prosper you and not to harm you, plans to give you hope and a future. If the main objective for both parties is not to contribute to growth, success, wellness and support of one another, then go to the Father in prayer. Ask what the purpose is for this particular relationship? Afterward, allow Him to guide you to your next step forward and sometimes out of that which may be blinding, hindering or distracting you.

Secondly, and referring to this same verse, how many of you are willing to go seeking at midnight (your darkest hour or time of need), in order to find aid to meet someone else's need? Believe it or not, doing so, can be likened to taking a stupendous leap and making a huge declaration of your faith. Are you willing to travel that extra mile, going over and above (boldly, barefoot, cold, alone and suffering) unselfishly (this may be our challenge) in order to bless and comfort someone else (whether stranger, friend, guest in our home or enemy)? Will you persevere and travail for someone else in prayer and petition before the Lord, or will your prayers continue to be selfish and self-righteous like the Pharisees?

Last but not least, who's door will you knock on in times such as these? Your Friend or a friend? Please be advised that, according to Matthew 25:40, "The King will reply, 'truly I tell you, whatever you did (or did not do) for one of the least of these brothers and sisters of mine; you did for me.' Thus, in order for your breakthrough to occur, you must be made slain to self, sadness, suffering and become active in your pursuit of opportunities to bless others.

In verse six the Holy Spirit asked me another direct question. How many people will feel comfortable or privileged enough to come to you on their journey (spiritual or faith walk) in order to find peace (rest and reassurance in Me)? Your honest answer to this question should also serve as a guide to the next steps that you will take. He then asked, when it is time to witness, how many of you feel as though you have nothing of sustenance to give? Does this feeling lead you to get on your feet to find someone else (a friend), more qualified? In all actuality, you should be prompted to get on your knees and go to the Lord (your Friend) in prayer? Then He said, I lead them to you so that you both would seek Me. Tip: when witnessing, it's simple. Speak nothing but the truth on how He has blessed and continues to sustain you.

In verse seven, He asks, "in your time of need, were you treated and answered inappropriately? If so, how did or would you respond? Do you bare the same resemblance (way of thinking) as most? Meaning, are you attempting to fit into the eye of the needle or still trying to blend into the back with the crowd? Do you still try to fight fire with fire, when water (the Living Water) should be our only option and means of survival?

Keep in mind that, the way that others treat you could be a direct reflection on how they treat themselves. At times, the mistreatment that you have received is more so about them, than it is about us. The Holy Spirit says, that when "that" person (whoever it was that you felt would and was in a position that they could bless you) refused to get up and answer the door (your call for help), that it hurt (both parties) but it was not about you. He showed me that in essence, they were saying, "I refuse to rise up from my current situation (comfort zone) or position (of unproductiveness) in order to bless anyone else. "My door (heart) is now shut" meant that this person was not open to being or partaking in a blessing. Therefore, their door remained closed and improperly positioned to receive the influx of blessings from Him for blessing you.

For this reason, verse eight should be very encouraging. It is now one of my favorite scriptures! The Holy Spirit said, I admonish you to persevere!" Regardless of how they treat or respond to you, do not do what seems easiest and give up in your time of need. Do not retreat or accept defeat as your alias. I need for you to progress, pursue and proceed by the power of the Holy Spirit resting within you. Most people know and have memorized the acronym PUSH (Pray Until Something Happens), but the Holy Spirit is commanding us to PUSSH like our very life depends on it! The meaning is simple, yet powerful. He is commanding us to "Pray Until a Significant Shift Happens" and the evidence is palpable.

The Holy Spirit then revealed to me that there are still too many of us who want the glory and the celebration of giving birth without having to struggle or go through the pain. This is not so. In addition to this, He said, "some of you are unaware why you are experiencing pain, anxiety, increased stress, a sense of urgency and the need to PUSSH." Well, it is very simple. You, my dear, are in the delivery room and about to give birth to the purpose of this pain. He invited me in to be privy to this fact, "This is all a part of the process. There is no way around it. Your life and purpose depend on your ability and willingness to PUSSH."

The Holy Spirit also showed me that He has intentionally placed some of you in the best birthing position (hardships that cause you to seek and recklessly rely solely on Him), and yet many are still trying to resist giving birth. You are kicking, complaining and going against the grain that He has picked for you. He likened it to being in active labor and refusing to push. This will only delay you somewhat, but you will give birth. You, my love, are only causing more pain, suffering, injury and stress on you and your "baby" (new aspect of self, purpose, newly found talents or spiritual gifts) that you are carrying. With this, I encourage you to put on the full armor of God (Ephesians 6) and embrace Deuteronomy 31:6 (Be strong and courageous, do not fear nor be afraid of them, for the Lord your God, He is the one that goes with you. He will not leave nor forsake you). But most importantly, you must PUSSH!

In verse nine, the Holy Spirit is asking us, "how do you ask?" Do you make your request known unto the Lord like we would for our children? Have you asked to find favor unto the Lord in the same fashion that you would present your husbands/wives with a "honey gone do list"? If so, you are demanding of the Lord, to operate the same way that you would. This only leaves no other option than to dismiss your requests until the appropriate changes are made in you.

In this same fashion, we must revisit two other areas. In seeking, what fashion are we presenting ourselves to others and Him? Are we secretly (ashamed of our relationship or lack thereof with Him) or underhandedly (selfishly and greedily) seeking of the Lord to act on our behalf? If so, this shall not work. He will not be able to prevail due to the contents of our contaminated hearts if this is the case. Are you knocking and then waiting for an answer? Are you so determined and self-righteous that you come at the Lord like a raging (deserving) bull, kicking the door in? If any of these depictions resemble your likeness, repent now.

Even in giving of our very best, there will be times in our lives that it still appears that we have no fruit to bear. It is at this time that I encourage you to repeat the process of asking, seeking and knocking. Begin with asking the Lord if it is your belief that hinders you. Do you believe that the Word is life (sustenance) and applicable to you and every situation that you are faced with? Do you believe that God is able to do all things but fail? Remember that He is the Creator of creation and spoke creation into being without parting His lips. This being said and accepted, means that your greatest challenges are not grand enough to challenge or confuse Him. Praise God. The answer could also be to wait. Maybe you have not persevered long enough.

Verse ten is our blessed reassurance. I will repeat it here. Verse ten, "for everyone (anyone, no exceptions, you and LaTrice) who asks receives, and he who seeks finds, and to him that knocks it (answers, mysteries, freedom) will be opened (unlocked, exposed, made free and available). My question to you is, are you an open and willing vessel? Are you willing to pick up your cross daily and follow Him so closely that others cannot tell where He stops, and you begin? Are you capable (willing) to forgive and love upon those that have hurt you the worst?

Keep in mind that this is exactly what He does for us every time that we come to the Lord in prayer. We have betrayed, denied and hurt Him immensely, and yet, He still loves, cares for and protects us. Ask Him to help you to recover from what condemns and corrupts your heart. Ask Him to teach you to love effortlessly and freely in the likeness of Him. Ask Him to help you to break free from the untruth, victimization and mental cages that could have (but has not) crippled you. Ask the Lord your God to show you how to pick up your sickbed and walk in freedom from this day forward.

Prayer

Heavenly Father, we come to you on this day in celebration of who you are. You are our victory, freedom, safety and strength. Lord, we love you. Father, we praise you right here in the midst of all that we go through. Lord, we ask you to speak to our hearts right here and now. Allow us to know what to say, where to go and what to do

Lord, for we are at a loss at times. We know that we can always turn and look to you. Lord, I ask that you baptize me in your Holy Spirit. Show me how to make you the very center upon which all things revolve. Allow me to be cleansed and purged of my sinful nature so that I can remain blameless in your sight. Fill me with your love towards others, cover me with the precious blood of the Lamb that was slain on my behalf from this day forth. Teach me how to mirror your walk here on earth from day to day Lord. Make intercession for me and set this captive free, in Jesus mighty, matchless and holy name.

Amen.

Chapter Seven
"COMPLETION"

Many of us are in a rush to hit the mark, cross the finish line, be at peace or feel complete. In essence, we are screaming, "Lord, I don't want to end up last." Well, the truth of the matter is that completion can seem to take an unprecedented amount of time, when you are the one hoping, wishing, crying (out loud or in silence) and praying for release. However, we must always remember to patiently press forward, trusting and believing God for our very best to arrive on schedule and without delays.

Being mindful that, what has brought us here (to our current state of being), more than likely, did not just manifest overnight, is imperative. "This," epidemic that we face or war that we rage against, more than likely, was shaped over an extended period of time. With that being said, we must wait heavily and defiantly upon the Lord in order to attain our healing, deliverance and breakthrough. This is not a chase that we run with or for other people. We must persist in obedience as we remain still and activate our active listening for the Holy Spirit's utterance.

In order to attain our victory, freedom or be covered with completion, we must first realize that we cannot achieve it on our own. One of the most arduous tasks that many of us will ever encounter is the one leading us to freedom from a mindset riddled with chains, a heart colored by brokenness and a spirit saturated with defeat. Trying to break free on our own can be likened to running as hard and as fast as you can towards your desired destination. Realizing, in the final moments, that you have a choke chain fastened around the collar of your neck.

This just may be how some of you view life. That your desired end continues to prove to be perfectly plain and insight but completely and utterly out of reach. Feeling as though you have constantly been choked slammed as you have attempted to maneuver forward, is what is meant by being lame in the feet. You may feel as though your only answer has been a consistent "no." For example, there is *no* viable escape, *no* end to the turmoil that you face and *no* reason to endure in this struggle any further. It may feel as though the wind has been kicked, snatched and knocked out of you. But God!

I know Him as my restorer, provider and strength. He has a way of making all things that we have suffered from in the past well worth the weight (pressure and heaviness that we have been carrying) and your wait (particular time frame or stay). Matthew four, verses one through four, speaks perfectly of this.

Verse one says, then Jesus was led up (believe it or not, He was chosen for this experience and so were you) of the (Holy) **Spirit** into the wilderness (place of confusion, waste, darkness, oblivion and/or hardship) to be tempted (bated, enticed, mocked, set up or fooled) of the devil. Verse two says, "and when he had fasted forty days and forty nights, he was afterward a hungered (hungry, thirsty, weakened or vulnerable state due to His obedience and sacrifice. Not because He had done something wrong. As a matter of fact, He did everything right. Some of the things that we go through are for no other reason than, it is written.

Verse three says, "and when the tempter (your enemy, abuser and the antagonist to your faith) came to Him, he said, If thou be the Son of God (if you are who you proclaim to be in Jesus), command that these stones be made bread." He, being your adversary, is mocking you. He is demanding that you, "prove it! Take these stones (things that are plentiful, insignificant and surrounding you) and use them to satisfy your needs and desires. He's trying to coerce you to do these things in your own power and according to your will which subtly demolish your dependence on God.

Satan is now utilizing your circumstance in an attempt to confuse and cause you to forget your sustenance (God). He is now attacking and provoking you by saying stop your agony (heartache, depression, anxiety and fill the void that you are faced with every day) instantaneously. If and when this does not happen, you will have then created just enough room for him to torment you even further. Please be advised that our opposition is a sly, slithery and strategic serpent. However, the Lord our God has positioned us with both favor and dominion over all things. He has made us triumphant and granted us the ability to staple satan up under our feet. The key to not getting ensnared by the wiles of the enemy is to remain vigilant. Trust, seek, adhere to God and remember that satan disguises himself as an angel of light (2 Corinthians 11:14).

Verse four, "but he (Jesus) answered and said, It is written, man shall not live by bread alone, but by every word that proceeded out of the mouth of God." So now, I ask you, do you know what the Living Word of God says about you? According to Isaiah 43:2, When you (place your name here) pass through the waters (troublesome times that will attempt to drown you), I (the Holy Spirit) will be with you; And through the rivers (per symbolism.org, irreversible passage of time possessing a sense of loss and oblivion), they shall **not** overflow you. When you walk through the fire (judgment, abuse, wrath, persecution and/or suffer from suicidal or homicidal attempts on your life), you shall not be burned (bear the resemblance of your attack), Nor shall the flame (intense pain, devise for destruction) scorch (devour or kill) you. Praise God!

In addition, Romans chapter five, verses one through four says, "therefore, having been justified by faith, we have peace with God through our Lord Jesus Christ, through whom also we have access by faith into this grace in which we stand, and rejoice in hope of the glory of God. And not only that, but we also glory in tribulations, knowing that tribulation produces perseverance; and perseverance, character; and character, hope."

For this reason, the Holy Spirit said to me that we all should be adding daily. In short, this means that our spiritual growth is and will remain to be continuous throughout our lives. We more than likely, will not receive "it" (wisdom, peace, patience, freedom, godliness, etc.) all in one setting. Sometimes, some things that are lost will ultimately equate to our gain. There will always be something or another that we struggle with as we are not perfect neither are, we all-knowing.

But the question is, do you have a coachable spirit? Are you willing to humble yourself and be purged to the point of emptiness? Will you grant Him full access in order to orchestrate a deep cleaning and reset on your belief system? Are you ready to take a step back and allow the Holy Spirit to facilitate your setup with triumph?

Sometimes, we have to remove ourselves in totality in order to be repositioned and realigned to experience the move of God. This may mean that a stealthy portion of our way of thinking, may have to be retracted as He shifts our position so that we can attain His view. But what are you in expectation of and who are you looking to for counsel? Your Friend or your friends?

To go even further, the Holy Spirit has shown me a vision on the analogy that we should all be adding daily. I saw a brown paper bag sitting on a kitchen counter. Someone (a hand) was trying to organize the contents secured inside. They continued to pull one thing out, present it before God, then it would immediately be replaced with something else.

For instance, I heard, "Remove fear, doubt and worry. This may take a while and quite a bit of practice in patience as you begin placing your faith in Me. But you and I can do it together." There was some shifting taking place inside the bag, even when I could not see it. This was followed by an elongated but plausible momentary silence that accompanied the wrestling taking place. "Now, replace it and fill the void with hope, increased faith and My joy. Reorganize. Now, remove impatience, anger and unforgiveness.

Those things are right at the surface. But if you dig a little deeper, you will discover hate as well. No. You may not see it at first, but trust me, it's there. This germ is hidden beneath your surface issues. One must conclude that removal of this nuisance is going to require quite a bit of time and effort. Removal of hate at the very root is quintessential to your success. Otherwise, like a perennial, it will continue to reoccur and choke out any seeds planted in your life. Once this is extracted, stand erect. Reorganize. Now add to your strengths, perseverance."

As this visual ended, I asked Him, "why the kitchen?" His answer was simple. The Holy Spirit enlightened me yet again, "this is where most perceive that they get their intake or fuel for life." Hallelujah. However, the truth of the matter is that we gain most of our (spiritual) intake, not in the food that we eat but the words, beliefs and attitudes that we ingest daily.

With or without our awareness or consent at times, consumption takes place. The music that we listen to, the movies that we watch and the conversations that we entertain, creates or destroys our values and belief systems. Be mindful of this at all times. The Holy Spirit has warned me in the past that some of the music that we engage in could be likened to eating gunpowder, popping a Viagra or playing a game of Russian Roulette. And then we still have the audacity, to wonder why we are always angry, consistently on arousal or to the point of extremeness in our depression.

Beware. Some of the most popular music today, should come with a childproof seal and warning labels attached like the ones found at the bottom or end of pharmaceutical advertisements. Be careful or you will become the direct reflection of your daily selections and subscriptions. If, by chance, this was the case, ask yourself, what would I look and smell like? What would I (insert name) represent?

If you would not be an accurate representation of His unparalleled promises and faithfulness towards us, repent. Changing your preferences and your playlist, can and will change and cause a great impact on your life. First Peter, chapter two verse nine says, "but you are a chosen generation, a royal priesthood, a holy nation, His own special people, that you may proclaim the praises of Him who called you out of darkness into His marvelous light." You were born to eradicate the darkness. Why then have you chosen to be planted in and surrounded by that which opposes your likeness to Him?

In order to answer the call and begin adding daily, some of us will have to begin with subtracting from any and all things that have been distracting or preventing us from coming into His presence. God could, but more than likely will not, saturate an environment that is already full of what is displeasing and contradictory unto Him. However, we still have a choice and the opportunity. As long as you draw breath in your body, it is never too late to pick up your cross and follow Christ.

When He wakes you up in the morning, say thank you and begin singing His praises. Ask Him to make sure that it is not just a physical occurrence and begin to believe, with all of your heart, that this awaking was both intentional and your spiritual awakening as well. Romans ten, verses nine and ten says, "that if you confess with your mouth the Lord Jesus and believe in your heart that God has raised Him from the dead, you will be saved." For with the heart, one believes unto righteousness, and with the mouth, confession is made unto salvation.

This leads me to the next question. What have you allowed your mouth to confess (declare and decree), in the past over yourself and others? Keep in mind that whether you were merely repeating the words of a song or recanting the lines from a movie, life or death has gone forth. Those words may have left a residual in your heart and spirit, which could later be silently imitated in your walk. However, you have the right and a way to change the course of your future. When you repent (admit to your faults and work to remove and restore any deficits), begin to believe that you are free from bondage and cleansed by the precious blood of the Lamb, and you are.

Once you are made free, lean to Him to remain there. There is no longer any reason to continue moving forward as you face towards what is progressively becoming a part of your past. Do an about face (radical turn), in and through Him. Philippians four verse thirteen says, "I can do all things through Christ who strengthens me." The question is, have you allowed Him to be your rock (solid foundation), strength (power, leverage and endurance) and protection (defense, immunity, assurance and coverage)?

Proverbs eighteen verse ten says, "the name of the Lord is a strong tower (take this time out, to define strong tower); the righteous run to it and are safe." Do you feel safe? If not, ask yourself, where is the place that I have chosen and continue to run to? Remember, although some things appear beneficial, they just may be a temporary facade in our here in now. You must also conclude that some of those very things may present the hindrance in our permanence and faith.

Speaking of which, I am led to ask you another important question. Are you secure in your faith and His faithfulness? Are you cognizant of what is required in order for you to transition unto the next platform or delve into a new dimension in Him? If you are not aware, simply ask. All of your needed changes can and will happen, but more than likely will be demanding of your time, willingness and ability to be likened to a client receiving a range of motion exercise.

This notion is not as complicated as it may seem at first. As a matter of fact, it's quite contrary to that. Your participation will demand that you are both active and aware of what is being required of you at any moment. In addition, there will be times that you will have no other option (due to pain, lack of ability/knowledge or the potential to cause more harm to injury) than to remain passive. Performing certain moves or shifts will be totally out of our hands and only able to be performed by Him. He alone is God. In these instances, He will lead us to be quiet, still and attentively awaiting His next instruction.

During these moments, He places us in a perfect position to receive what is therapeutic to our souls. He will never need our assistance, approval or advice. In all actuality, He never needed us, so we should marvel at the fact that He treats us as if He does. Additionally, He is the only one that has a history of breathing creation into being and still very capable of making massive miracles occur within a blink of an eye. Thus, we must be both adamant and willing to follow wherever our Father leads.

Last but not least, there may be another type of opportunity presented to you. In order for you to conclude with a therapeutic resolve, you may have to engage in your growth and development as someone receiving active-assisted activities or movements. To produce meticulous, coordinated and fluent movements, we must rest fully in Him. When you allow Him to choreograph your next movements and steps forward, without resistance, is to prove Him to be the Author and Finisher of your faith (Hebrews 12:2).

It is with this opportunity that I implore you to seek him with every essence of your being. Hebrews chapter eleven, verse six, is very promising. It states this: "but without faith it is impossible to please Him, for he who comes to God must believe that He is, and that He is a rewarder of those who diligently seek Him." Do you not want to gain access to your reward? If so, offer Him you in totality. Your heart, life, broken places, the darkest desires that constrain you to a life of shame and remorse are His to treasure, refine and enhance.

When we give broken pieces of ourselves (grief, loneliness, heartache, fearfulness or hate) unto Him, leave them there. Invite Him in and permit Him to do the necessary repairing and replacing. Learning to trust the process, especially when it appears that you have no reason to, is a paramount part of achieving your exponential growth. Knowing that His grace is sufficient as His love covers and makes us whole, is the key to making our very foundation impenetrable.

In this same token, we have to be willing to (actively) reach for the goals in which we plan to attain and utilize.

When it pertains to pursuing our faith and securing our belief for our peace, prosperity, freedom and healing, we can no longer be reactive (waiting for something spontaneous to happen) for release to occur. We must be proactive (the cause of) your breakout and breakthrough taking place. Matthew 17:21, However, this kind does not go out except by prayer and fasting. With that being said, I'll install both the period and the adjacent question mark here. When was the last time that you fasted?

Well, the sad part and very real truth is that many of us have never actually participated in a true fast. If I am allowed to be real for a moment pertaining to this topic, many of us have only followed the crowd and leaned to "their" (leadership, tradition and religious practices) understanding of it. However, on this day, I ask you to be willing to change your current thoughts and impractical practices used to please an all-knowing God. I strongly encourage you to do the research for yourself. Find out not only what it means to fast (Biblical significance), find out what you are and are not to do and begin doing the like.

Secondly, identify what your expected outcomes are. After this, place them firmly, in the hands of God. Remember, the more ridiculous your belief (that God can and will do it), the more radical your faith. Glory to God!

Moreover, it is just as important for you to know what will take place without a sound understanding of fasting. Without this pertinent knowledge, we more than likely have participated in a mass or even sole starvation attempt. To secure a close relationship with God, gain His wisdom or possess His peace in the face of defeat, there are both specific and intentional steps that we must take. These actions will, in fact, allow you to achieve your desired goals, as long as you are being led for the right (not selfish) reasons.

And contrary to popular opinion, to merely give up food does not constitute fasting. It does not bear the same resemblance as to offer up a true sacrifice (time, focus and meditation) of your heart. It can't be classified as being holy (without blemish, dedication to worship/honor and serve our King). Starving yourself, for any length of time, cannot be compared to picking up your cross daily in constant pursuit of pursuing the very presence of God. Fasting, my friends, is our attempt to allow God and others to see Jesus through the course of our actions, not the words that we speak. It is to be spiritually acceptable (agreeable, pleasing) unto God.

In addition to this, how is your heart? We must first realize that it's condition must be examined not just daily, but throughout the course of our day. We must ask and seek to find out the true reason or hidden agenda for everything that we do. For example, sometimes we (self-included) tend to do what appears to be right for the very wrong reasons. However, we have the right and have been afforded the opportunity to go before God.

Surrender. Adhere. Allow. These are the words that He has spoken for me to utilize and then advance towards you. These words may possess the power of release over the strongholds in your life. Attaining a sense of completion from the pain paralyzing your future endeavors and joy may require you to apply all three words liberally and without debate. This may be the integral piece that was missing and preventing you from breaking free of the chains straddling your mindset.

Furthermore, in order to secure our sense of completion, we must come to the realization that in our fasting, we must *only* be seeking Him. Any and everything else is the icing on the best cake ever presented. Honor Him not by your lip service, but by spending your precious time in fellowship with Him. Second Peter one verses two through eight says, "grace and peace be multiplied to you in the knowledge of God and of Jesus our Lord, as His divine power has given to us all things that pertain to life and godliness, through the knowledge of Him who called us by glory and virtue, by which have been given to us exceedingly great and precious promises, that through these you may be partakers of the divine nature, having escaped the corruption that is in the world through lust. But also, for this very reason, giving all diligence, add to your faith virtue, to virtue knowledge, to knowledge self-control, to self-control perseverance, to perseverance godliness, to godliness brotherly kindness, and to brotherly kindness love. For if these things are yours and abound, you will be neither barren nor unfruitful in the knowledge of our Lord Jesus Christ."

After reading these verses, The Holy Spirit softly asks, "are you (add your name here) adding up (in your Kingdom contributions)? Are you spending your time blessing others through your gift of giving (time, kindness, empathy, finance, hope, discipleship and forgiveness)? If you continue to give, especially in your season of systematic delinquencies, there is an abundant blessing in that. This may indeed be where you encounter your healing or achieve His peace in your life.

Remember, there is power in perception or how we interpret things to be. So, here is another question personally addressed to you. Are you continuing to count your blessings or consistently itemizing your afflictions? If you continue to seek (looking for it to be there), proclaim (speak it over your life) and settle for (verses wrestle with) defeat, it will always be there.

She (being defeat) will stare and pin you down (mentally, spiritually and physically) instead of or until you cast her out, by name. Let defeat know that your life is not her final resting place. Say, "I command every contrite, broken and venomous spirit of to be made slain in Jesus' name. Defeat, you are no longer welcome here and are rebuked off of my life in the precious and mighty name of Jesus. I am free.

According to John 8:36, if the Son makes you free, you shall be free indeed. Now, let's take a slight pause in order to comprehend this. We, You (name insert) and I, have the victory in Christ. Declare it over your life, family, friends and enemies as well. The Holy Spirit promises that "as you do the adding, I will then do the multiplying in your life. Sometimes this is accomplished in accordance with our faith. Can "this," your lack of faith, be what has hindered your breakthrough? If so, ask your Heavenly Father to disengage, dismantle and disenfranchise what has disabled your faith.

My question to you is do you believe that in God, all things are made possible? Is He all that you need, period or are there still some if and or buts attached to this statement? Do you have a relationship with Him? Are you truly trusting and seeking Him, wholeheartedly on a daily basis? When your heart is hurting, can you surrender your all unto Him?

I implore you to cry out unto your Heavenly Father. Even though He is waiting patiently for you, I know that it could very well prove to be one of the hardest things to do. I recently visited a church and felt an urge in my spirit to be cleansed. There was a tugging within to wail at the altar to drop to my knees and cry out unto the Lord like never before.

Contrarily, I held it in as much as I could. Feeling as if this action and my blatant disobedience was only suffocating me harder and potentially stifling my progression forward, and yet I could not let go. My body began to shake vehemently, and my tear ducts felt as if they were swelling painfully in the back of my throat as a squeal continued to be expelled from deep within. I struggled to remain in control of myself and maintain both my dignity and composure.

After all of these years, it was hard for me to cry or appear to be weak, even before my King.

The Holy Spirit continued to urge me, and I am now sharing it with you, "Let go." He told me, "See, right here and now, you are attempting to handle this on your own, refusing to allow Me to reign in this situation. This is what is keeping you in bondage. When you (I) release the wail that is trapped within, it will be the day of the total release of power and control unto Me.

Release it all to God. Take the things that you have been struggling with: the hideousness of the crime(s) against you, the broken and bitterness of your heart, the scar tissue (the residual of your abuse), the shame and every other title that you have been answering to. Take them off now and refuse to ever wear them again. Like a sweater, as I give each thing to God, I literally act as if I am taking them off and pull them over my head. I then do the same actions in reverse.

I then begin to place the discontinued items onto God, one garment at a time. I then say, "here Lord are the things that I harbor in my heart. Take this brokenness. I cast it onto you Lord, I cannot handle it on my own." I repeat this process with each item until I feel a release or weight being lifted. You can and should do the same. It may feel ridiculous at first, so I advise you to do this in the secrecy of your prayer closet.

Be ye reminded that, 1 Corinthians 13:11 says, "when I was a child, I spoke as a child, I understood as a child, I thought as a child: but when I became a man, I put away childish things." In this particular case we are talking about your freedom, your life and your destiny. It is time to put away the brokenness, frustration and hurt. Lay them to rest by casting them at His feet by name continuously, if need be. See yourself walking away and never looking back at the cage that once caressed you to the point of decreased consciousness.

Can you see yourself as free and abused no more? The Lord of Host is waiting for you to declare this over your life. The chains have been broken, peace is yours and all you have to do is surrender these things unto your Master, Creator and Friend. He is there with open arms waiting to offer you His forgiveness, peace and the joy in knowing that He has never left nor forsaken you. Your past, present and future sins are already known about and forgiven. Will you accept His offer on this day and be free? The choice, opportunity and season is yours for the taking. Completion is here. All you have to do is humble yourself, release all that was never yours to begin with, pray for yourself and those that have hurt you.

Now believe and repeat aloud, John 19:30. Jesus said, "it is finished." My season of abuse, brokenness, and recluse is complete. I am made free in Jesus name I pray.

Amen.

Abused No More

"The Breaking Of A Mindset"

Made in the USA
Columbia, SC
02 July 2020

11724717R00059